BRITAIN IN OLD PHOTOGRAPHS

THE CHANGING FACE OF
CROYDON

CHRISTINE CORNER

CROYDON LOCAL STUDIES LIBRARY
SUTTON PUBLISHING LIMITED

Sutton Publishing Limited
Phoenix Mill · Thrupp · Stroud
Gloucestershire · GL5 2BU

First published 1999

Title page photograph: Garden at 'Clevelands', Eldon Park, South Norwood, April 1908.

British Library Cataloguing in Publication Data
A catalogue record for this book is available from the British Library.

ISBN 0-7509-1545-5

Typeset in 10.5/13.5 Photina.
Typesetting and origination by
Sutton Publishing Limited.
Printed in Great Britain by
Ebenezer Baylis, Worcester.

For Mum

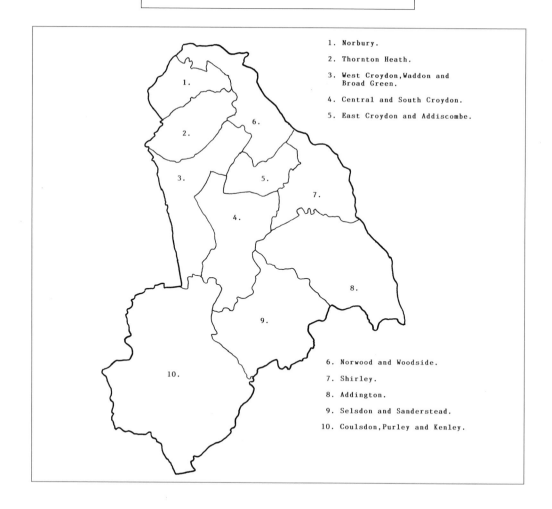

1. Norbury.

2. Thornton Heath.

3. West Croydon, Waddon and Broad Green.

4. Central and South Croydon.

5. East Croydon and Addiscombe.

6. Norwood and Woodside.

7. Shirley.

8. Addington.

9. Selsdon and Sanderstead.

10. Coulsdon, Purley and Kenley.

CONTENTS

Shirley Windmill, October 1916. Shirley Mill is situated on the west side of Upper Shirley Road. In 1910 a post-mill was built and leased to William Alwen and his family, who were the original millers of Shirley. In 1854 the mill was destroyed in a fire and the second, still existing mill, with a brick tower, was built on the site. During the First World War the mill was used for storing linen. Croydon Corporation bought the land by compulsory purchase for John Ruskin School in 1951, and the school was demolished in the early 1990s.

INTRODUCTION

This second volume of old Croydon photographs reflects a changing society within living memory and focuses on aspects of life in the borough when the pace was a little less frantic. By the turn of the century the rapid expansion of Croydon was well under way. In 1896 Croydon had a new, larger and in every way more impressive Town Hall in Katharine Street, in keeping with its status as a County Borough. North End and George Street were already developing into shopping areas and other local shopping centres were coming into being as the town was becoming ever more populous. Croydon is still the largest commercial and retail centre in the south-east outside the capital, although there is more competition than ever before from new shopping complexes. In the first decades of the century the well-known department stores of Allders, Grants and Kennards were the main attraction for visitors from miles around.

By the 1930s Purley Way had been opened as a relief road to divert traffic away from the congestion already occurring in the town centre. The bypass was also planned to serve the new Croydon Airport terminal buildings. These included the Aerodrome Hotel, which is now the Post House. After many years as an airport of global importance, Croydon closed in 1959. Purley Way changed its character to become an industrial landscape of gas works and factories in the post-war years. The contemporary Purley Way has now become a traffic black spot itself, as motorists flock to visit the retail superstores which flank the road.

The Second World War had a great impact on civilian life and Croydon was very badly bombed. It was the town in the south-east that was worst hit in Doodlebug raids. Following the war, there was a housing shortage and areas of farmland around the town were used for building, while many Victorian mansions were demolished or converted into flats for multi-occupation. However, post-war Croydon looked much as it had and the Croydon Corporation Act, passed in 1956 (when the council obtained powers enabling it to develop a large part of the town centre), led to the building of huge office blocks which shaped Croydon's future through the ensuing decades. The initial success of Croydon's development as a business centre was in line with the government's policy of encouraging businesses to move out of central London. In 1965 Croydon's population rose significantly when Coulsdon and Purley Urban District Council was absorbed into the London Borough of Croydon. In recent years, since the 1970s, there has been a reverse in the trend for urbanisation and depopulation of the countryside, as people have begun to move out to the rural areas once more. Commuters are travelling increasing distances to work and many of Croydon's workforce come from Kent, Sussex and north of the Thames.

Much of Croydon's built heritage has been lost since 1945, some fine examples including Whitgift School (demolished to make way for the Whitgift Centre), the Shirley Park Hotel, the Davis and Grand Theatres and St Matthew's Church in George Street. In recent years there has been a major shift in attitude towards a recognition of the need for the active preservation and conservation of structures like Shirley Windmill and buildings within the recently designated Local Areas of Special Character, including Birdhurst Road, Church Street and the Norbury Estate.

With the advent of television came the decline of mass attendances at processions, carnivals and other leisure events within the borough. Thankfully, Croydon's wealth of parks and its green spaces were saved from development and remain one of the borough's greatest assets. The Council has designated Conservation Areas, including such diverse places as Bradmore Green and South Norwood High Street, which should be protected from adverse development. The Fairfield Halls were built in 1962 and they remain a popular entertainment venue. It is just across the road from Croydon's newest cultural complex, Croydon Clocktower, which houses the Central Library, the David Lean Cinema, Lifetimes Museum and Croydon Tourist Information Centre, and has its own arts workshops, exhibition galleries and shop. Croydon still maintains a high profile as an important centre for leisure and entertainment.

Croydon has always had excellent road and rail links with London and the south-east, and these can only be enhanced if proposals for a London Underground rail extension to the borough come to fruition. The first trams since 1951 are set to run in Croydon as the Tramlink Project nears its completion at the time of writing. Hopes are high that the first modern, environmentally friendly tram system in the south of England can help to solve some of Croydon's traffic congestion problems. As we approach the millennium, Croydon has the opportunity to apply for city status once again. People's perceptions of the town have often been of a 'concrete jungle' with no soul, but Croydon appears to be going through another period of transition in order to shake off the shackles of its 1960s image and move forward with optimism into the next century.

ACKNOWLEDGEMENTS

I would like to express my grateful thanks to the following for their help in the compilation of this book:

The staff of Croydon Local Studies Library, Steve Roud and Margaret Mumford and the borough's archivist, Steve Griffiths; the staff at Purley Public Library; John Gent for generously allowing me to use photographs from his collection; Mr R. Misson for his help with captions; Ian Currie for information on local weather conditions; staff at the Imperial War Museum for advice; and Ron Corner and Liz Hollowood for their encouragement and support. Most of the photographs in this book have been selected from the collection of over 40,000 at Croydon Local Studies Library and the smaller collection at Purley Public Library. Thanks are offered in particular to the following for giving permission to reproduce their photographs, with apologies for any omissions: Mrs E. Baker, Miss D. Bliss, Miss B. Cocksedge, *The Croydon Advertiser*, Croydon Natural History and Scientific Society, Mrs T. Flemming, Mr D. Garman, Mr John Gent, Mrs J. Holman, Mr A. Holmes, Miss D. Iceton, Mr P. Johnstone, Mr R. Lewis, Mrs E. Luxton, Mr T. Miller, Mr R. Misson, Mr G. Morris, Mr F. Paine, Mr C. Reeves, Mr J. Rickard, Mr G. Rollason, Mr B. Royal, Mr A.J.C. Saunders, Mrs B. Smith, the Steel family, Mrs M. White, Dr M. Williams, Mrs C. Wilson.

If anyone can supply more information concerning any of the pictures (and of any errors which may have occurred!) please let the staff at Croydon Local Studies Library know. Finally, I should like to add that this book contains a purely personal selection of photographs. In particular I have tried to choose those which might jog people's memories of times past in and around Croydon within the last sixty years or so.

CHAPTER ONE

NORBURY

Norbury Farm House, as seen from the Southern Railway Line, c. 1905. The farm was originally the mansion house for the manor of Norbury and stood approximately where Kensington and Norbury Avenues meet. It was demolished in 1914.

Above is a view of Norbury Station building and the railway bridge, looking east from London Road, March 1961. In order for trams to run under the railway bridge the road had to be lowered in 1901, which explains the dip in the road. The present brick building of Norbury Station, shown below in1969, was not constructed until 1902. The original station, built in 1878, may have been known as Norbury Tower Station and was made of wood. The railway bridge was widened in 1902, following an application made to the Local Government Board for '. . . sanction to borrow the sum of £4,500'. The track was doubled at this time and by 1940 over 200 trains a day were calling at Norbury, which was becoming part of the busy commuter belt as it is today.

The firm of Smith Durham, London Road, Norbury, 1921. The family firm of Smith Durham opened their menswear shop in 1904. The business began as a partnership between James Smith and his friend, Freddie Durham, and traded in Norbury for almost a century. The shop closed in 1996 following a fall in trade, as people were shopping less in smaller centres where parking was becoming increasingly difficult.

Carson's Warehouse, 1355–7 London Road, April 1960. The emporium of Walter Carson and Sons Ltd, Paint Manufacturers and Exporters, was built in 1905 as the King Edward Hall, King Edward VII Parade. The premises were used as a Baptist church, c. 1908 and for Norbury skating rink, c. 1910. The building also housed Norbury Cinema from 1911 until 1937 when it fell victim to the competition from the Rex Cinema which opened at the beginning of that year. During the Second World War the premises became a 'British Restaurant', serving cheap meals. The building was gutted in the 1960s to become a supermarket.

Two very different views of Green Lane, some twenty years apart. The road developed from sixteen houses in 1914, at the time of the photograph above, to over 300 in the mid-1930s which is the date of the lower view. This ancient road dates back two thousand years to when it was a track in the forest, linked with the Great North Wood which became part of the first route from Croydon to London. The coming of trams and trains was the main factor in Norbury's development in the twentieth century, although until *c.* 1914 Norbury was still quite a rural suburb. In the inter-war years much building development took place and the present road pattern was established.

St Oswald's Road, December 1971. Trees are being felled in the grounds of St Oswald's church. Voluntary workers cut down twenty-two trees, which had been affected by Dutch Elm Disease, on the boundary of Thornton Heath and Norbury. Many more were felled in the 1930s during development.

No. 100 Northwood Road, formerly The Leather Bottle Inn, 1955. Northwood Road, which takes its name from the former Great North Wood, was known as Spa Road until 1911. The highway running into Spa Hill was previously known as Leather Bottle Lane. The Leather Bottle Inn has been a private residence since 1896.

Norbury Junior Library, *c.* 1946. Norbury Library opened in 1931, with a large children's area and even a lecture hall provided for 'educational lectures and slide shows'. The first junior library was housed temporarily in Norbury Manor School from 1930. By 1933 Croydon had the largest library system in the south of England and continues to sustain a heavy level of use, providing an acclaimed service to borough residents and visitors alike.

Norbury Manor Boys' School, with Peter Fletcher (former Head) at the demolition of the school in March 1987. The Stanford Road Senior Mixed School was opened in 1913 and renamed Norbury Manor in 1922. The school closed in 1986 because of falling rolls, and sheltered housing for the elderly was built on the site.

Norbury Brook, February 1975. Norbury Brook is an ancient stream, one of the tributaries of the River Wandle which first rises as the Norbury Brook in Addiscombe. It flows in a culvert through Thornton Heath, passes under Brigstock Road and then proceeds through Norbury, beside Norbury Park towards the Croydon/Lambeth border at Hermitage Bridge, London Road. At this point it changes its name to the River Graveney.

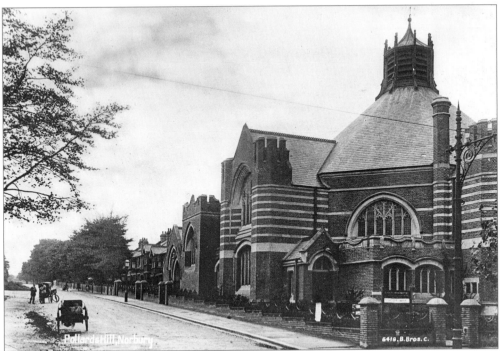

Wesleyan Chapel, Pollards Hill North, at the junction of London Road, 1909. The chapel was built in 1905 and later became Norbury Methodist Church, which was pulled down in 1977. There is still a Methodist Hall at the site today (behind the Health Centre) which is also a Pop-In Centre for the retired.

St Stephen's Church, Warwick Road, Norbury/Thornton Heath border, April 1960. St Stephen's Church dates from 1909. Its parishioners would formerly have attended an iron mission church, built in 1889, which seated a maximum of 250 people. St Stephen's is a Grade II listed church building and a perfect example of an Edwardian architect's vision.

A view from Pollards Hill recreation grounds, looking towards Mitcham Common, 1921. Pollards Hill occupies the highest point in Norbury and it is possible to see central Croydon, Epsom Downs, Mitcham Common and even Windsor Castle from here. The area was once part of the Great North Wood and was given to the council in 1913 by Sir Frederick Edridge, former mayor of Croydon.

Fields near Norbury Golf Course, looking east towards Beulah Hill, May 1923. Norbury Golf Club was situated at the western end of Stanford Road. At one time there were tennis, cricket and football clubs, as well as two golf links, in Norbury. Norbury Golf Club disappeared as a result of inter-war house building. Norbury's other course was the North Surrey Golf Course where Norbury Park now stands.

London Road at the Norbury/Thornton Heath border near Goldwell Road during the Second World War. London Road is deserted by today's standards, and there are white bands on the trees and lamp-posts to make it easier for people to find their way about during the blackout.

CHAPTER TWO

THORNTON HEATH

Thornton Heath Station, c. 1940. The first Thornton Heath Station building was known as Colliers Water Lane Station in 1862, New Thornton Heath in 1869 and finally Thornton Heath in the 1890s, when the station was completely rebuilt to its present more spacious design.

The opening of the new Thornton Heath fire station, along with the library, 8 July 1914, by the Mayor, Alderman Frank Denning, in the presence of Sir Frederick and Lady Edridge. The premises were designed to accommodate two fire engines (the station was given the first motorised vehicles) and provide living quarters for eight married firemen. There is a block of flats built in the late 1960s/early 1970s on the Chipstead Avenue corner site now.

An early postcard of Thornton Heath Library, which was opened in 1914 (along with the fire station), following a generous donation of £4,200 by library benefactor Andrew Carnegie. The original library was sited in Thornton Heath High Street in 1891, but soon became too small for the developing area. The library serves a diverse multi-cultural community today.

Whitehorse Road recreation ground, *c.* 1938, before the shelter was removed. The ground was acquired in 1891, with the purpose of providing an informal play area for local children who lived in a built-up neighbourhood. The main part of the field was used for ARP shelters during the Second World War.

Galpins Road, after a light fall of snow, looking over the golf links towards Mitcham from near Silverleigh Road, December 1925. The road was first laid out in 1881 but was not developed until around 1908, when the first houses were built at the London Road end.

Winterbourne Junior Girls' School visit to Paris, 1936. Winterbourne Girls' School opened in 1907 as a post-infants school in Winterbourne Road and was reorganised for Junior Girls only in 1932. Girls at the school have recently produced their own prize-winning promotional video.

Mayday Road Hospital nurses' annual sports, July 1927. Mayday Hospital was opened in 1885, with the Archbishop of Canterbury as guest of honour, as the Union Infirmary with 325 beds. A new nurses' home opened in 1931. Nurses had always been given some training at the hospital and in 1919 an official three-year course was implemented. It is now a university hospital with full teaching facilities.

Thornton Heath clocktower and High Street, late 1940s/early 1950s. The clocktower stands on the area of land formerly known as Walkers' Green. The council decided to build a public clock on this site after the green was fenced off because of its poor condition.

Brigstock Road, from the clocktower, Thornton Heath, 1953. A small Tesco store can be seen, and the largest Tesco in the London area opened on the corner of Parchmore Road in 1982. In recent years Thornton Heath centre had begun to show signs of neglect, but a programme of improvements to upgrade the High Street area, making it more attractive for residents, local businesses and shoppers, has been implemented.

Two views of Thornton Heath Pond, pre-1955, when it was filled in and in the process of being demolished. The concrete wall for the roundabout is being built inside the pond area to make room for the road widening which is to follow. The pond is thought to have been in existence since at least the Middle Ages, when it would have been used as a watering hole for livestock and horses. It was also used by local colliers or charcoal burners as a water supply.

CHAPTER THREE

WEST CROYDON, WADDON & BROAD GREEN

May Queen and procession at Waddon School, 1937.

St Michael and All Angels' Church, from the grounds of Wellesley House on the right, 1960. The Grade I listed church opened in 1881, services having originally been held in a temporary church from 1872. The building, which once dominated its immediate surroundings, is now hemmed in by West Croydon bus station and the Lloyds Register building. Wellesley House is first recorded in 1859 – it was once the residence of Jabez Spencer Balfour, Croydon's infamous first mayor. It was demolished around 1965.

The Fox and Hounds pub, London Road, late 1940s. The inn dates back to 1800, its predecessor being the Red Lion inn. In 1874, a John Goodman kept the premises and provided hunting facilities with an entrance in Derby Road leading to stables. The pub was rebuilt in the 1890s.

Concord House, the former West Croydon Congregational church and the Philips Electronics building, London Road, June 1992. West Croydon Congregational church opened in 1886, its 'tall and graceful spire' visible for many miles, but is now dwarfed by two towering office blocks. The church has now become a Jain Oshwal Centre.

Croydon General Hospital, new Outpatients' Department, March 1928. Croydon General Hospital was first established in 1866 with fourteen beds, and in 1873 the Archbishop of Canterbury performed the opening ceremony of the thirty-bed hospital on its present site in London Road. It was another Archbishop of Canterbury who opened the Outpatients Department in 1927, the ceremony being followed by an inspection by King George V and Queen Mary. The hospital closed its doors to patients for the last time in July 1996 and the future of the site is still uncertain.

A.H. Allen and Co. Ltd. Flour Mill, St James' Road, 1923. The firm of A.H. Allen and Co., Millers, has been in existence from the beginning of the twentieth century. When the mill closed down some of the forty-five employees, who lived in the row of cottages adjacent to the mill in Tavistock Grove, lost their homes, which were pulled down along with the mill. The site was earmarked for the Wonderloaf Bakery, which was probably the largest bakery in Europe in 1961. The automatic bakery was producing over 2,500 loaves an hour in its heyday, although it too has closed recently.

The Gillett and Johnston Clocktower, Union Road, decorated for peace celebrations at the end of the First World War. The firm of Gillett and Johnston established their bell foundry in 1844 and by 1868 had one of the first steam-powered clock factories in the world. The clocktower was added to the building as a working advertisement for their craft. At its peak the company had contracts in Canada, the USA and New Zealand. The works were closed down in 1957, following financial difficulties, and the foundry was demolished in 1997, leaving a heritage plaque to mark the site. The firm still operates from premises in South Croydon.

The Broadway, Whitehorse Road, 1924. Whitehorse Road took its name from Bensham Manor House, which was given to Walter Whitehorse and stood to the south-east of the junction of Whitehorse Road and Whitehorse Lane. After the coming of the railways to Croydon in the mid-nineteenth century, there was a period of rapid growth in house building, and Whitehorse Road began to develop into the busy thoroughfare it is today.

Harvesting at Waddon Court Farm, 1907, in the Station field on Stafford Road, opposite old Waddon Station. The old Manor House of Waddon Court was originally a medieval moated site. The area is now known as Waddon Ponds. Waddon Court was rebuilt in the late eighteenth century, and Lord Nelson is reputed to have been one of the notable visitors to the house who may have fished in the lakes there.

Prospect Place, Duppas Hill Lane, 1932.
Prospect Place was a row of cottages from
Duppas Hill Lane to Old Town and was
demolished in the 1940s. The area is
unrecognisable today, and Duppas Hill Lane
runs along next to the flyover which opened
in June 1969.

The junction of Canterbury Road and Wortley Road, c. 1910. Canterbury, Stanley and Boston
Roads were developed from the early 1850s in what had been the grounds of Weller House.
Wortley Road was renamed from Lower York Road in 1878. The firm of F. Musgrove, Baker, took
over from Robert Mead, Baker in 1901 and traded until 1921 when another baker, T. Brooks, took
over the business.

Bowmans, the Bakers, Mitcham Road, 1934. Mr R.L. Bowman began his bakery business in Southbridge Road in 1929 and retired in 1964, transferring the ownership and management of his six shops to his son-in-law, Mr J.W. Coughlan, who also had six shops at that time. Coughlan's shop is still there to this day.

Lombard Roundabout, showing Mitcham Road and Purley Way, 1955. A view of one of Croydon's busiest roundabouts, taking traffic to London and south to the coast, taken after the roundabout was completed. It was known locally as the 'Lombard' roundabout, after the Lombard Bank, which left the area in 1986 having been part of the local landscape since 1959. The cooling towers (demolished in the mid-1990s) were close to the Croydon 'B' power station, which was demolished in 1991 and is now the site of the IKEA furniture superstore.

Purley Way and Commerce Way from the roof of the Walls ice-cream depot, June 1961. The evening rush-hour shown here seems to consist of more pedestrians than traffic, in sharp contrast to how things are today! Purley Way was originally designed as a 'relief road', its purpose being to divert through-traffic away from Croydon's town centre. Several industrial concerns sited their factories on Purley Way, and the construction of a new power station in addition to the existing Croydon Gas Works made it Croydon's principal industrial district in the 1950s and 1960s.

The London to Brighton Veteran Car Rally, Purley Way, in the 1960s. In 1932 the southern section of the Purley Way became the first highway in Britain to be lit by the latest innovative sodium lighting. The system, which was extended along the entire length of the road in 1936, can be seen here showing the centrally suspended lamps, which were taken down about fifteen years ago.

CHAPTER FOUR

CENTRAL &
SOUTH CROYDON

The Green Dragon, in the High Street, one of Croydon's oldest coaching inns, was closed in 1959 to make way for the office block we know as Green Dragon House.

Park Lane, 1938. These large houses were between the footpath to Park Hill and Barclay Road. Like many other roads in the borough Park Lane has changed its name, having been known in the early years as Back Lane. It has always been a thoroughfare, although not always as busy as it is today.

Park Lane Underpass looking towards Wellesley Road, 1964/65.The underpass was opened in November 1964, two months ahead of its expected completion date. It carved a channel through the centre of Croydon and at the time of this picture work on the Fairfield forecourt was still in progress, with the car park undergoing an extension.

Wellesley Road, opposite the electricity showroom, 1936/37. The house is on the site of Norfolk House, an eleven-storey slab block extending round into George Street, which was built in 1958/9, one of the first major office developments to contribute to Croydon's 'Manhattan-style' skyline.

George Street, looking east from the Park Lane crossroads, 1956. The building with the clocktower is John Thrift & Sons Ltd, grocers and provision merchants, whose business was founded in Church Street in 1857. It outgrew its original premises and moved to George Street, then it was demolished in 1962 to permit road widening. The clock in the tower was formerly in the tower of the old Town Hall in the High Street.

High Street, 1914. A bustling scene showing trams, cyclists and a horse and cart, in addition to busy shoppers. The signs of the firms of Robinson's and Foley's can be seen advertising 'teeth', for which there was obviously a demand. The firm of Robinson's sold sets of teeth for twenty shillings and did painless extractions for one shilling! Harry Hawkins, on the corner of the present entrance to the Whitgift Centre, was a licensed victualler at the Croydon pub, number 37 High Street.

High Street Croydon looking north, 1956. The Davis Theatre was showing the controversial film *Rock Around The Clock* and was the only South London cinema to show the film on Sunday. Police were called to restore order when young people climbed onto the stage and danced in front of the screen. The Davis was the fourth largest cinema in Britain and a very popular entertainment venue for Croydonians. Declining audiences, following the impact of television, resulted in its closure in May 1959.

Scarbrook Road Swimming Baths, showing the large pool being demolished, 1974. Croydon's Central Swimming Baths opened in 1866, consisting of an outdoor swimming bath and a smaller covered bath. In 1910 publicity for the baths stated the outdoor bath was for 'gentlemen only in the summer months', which were classed as April to October. In 1965 a site was reserved in Barclay Road for a new Central Baths, the existing building being in need of considerable repair by this time. However, this was not to be, and when the building was demolished in 1974 the council was unable to afford the construction of new baths. Croydon still lacks a central swimming pool.

The Town Hall, Katharine Street, at the turn of the century, a short time after its opening in 1896. Croydon has had three town halls, the present building being completed in 1895, the second in 1808 and the first built in either 1566 or 1609, although there is some confusion as to the exact construction date. Charles Henman was the architect who designed the present building, and the local firm of Gillett and Johnston were commissioned to produce a clock and bells for the 176-ft tower, which no longer dominates the skyline as it once did (see page 26).

A fire at A.C. Ebbutt's Upholstery Workshops led to this damage to the Braithwaite Hall, Katharine Street, May 1905. This is now the site of the new Croydon Clocktower complex and was also home to the temporary library for some years between 1971 and 1990. Local newspaper reports at the time claimed that when the fire had been brought under control it had already got through the ventilators and into the Braithwaite Hall. This brought renewed calls for the construction of a new Central Fire Station which was opened in Park Lane at the end of 1906.

Croydon Town Hall from the air, c. 1932. The third of Croydon's Town Halls was opened in 1896, a large, grand structure reflecting the fact that Croydon had become a Borough. The Council Chamber and court rooms are still used for their original purpose, but nearly all the council departments are housed in Taberner House. The Braithwaite Hall, named after the vicar of Croydon Parish Church, contained the Reference Library and Information Centre, until the opening of the new Central Library in November 1993.

Browsing at the dealer and bookseller's at 60 Southbridge Road, *c.* 1950. Southbridge Road was originally known as Southbridge Lane and led to the South Bridge which was built over the River Wandle.

Surrey Street market looking north, 1957. The earliest records of a market in Croydon go back to 1276 when Archbishop Kilwardby obtained a Royal Charter for a weekly market. It is likely that a market existed before that time and the charter simply formalised the arrangement. Surrey Street market was held daily from the 1920s and in 1994 celebrated many years of trading with a royal visit by Prince Charles. It is one of Croydon's best known features and full of local colour.

Whitgift School playing fields, prior to bulldozing, autumn 1964. Viewed from Park Street, Wellesley Road is on the right and St Michael and All Angels' church is to the left. The Whitgift Foundation was set up in the reign of Elizabeth I by Archbishop Whitgift as a charitable organisation. The Whitgift School, built here in the mid-nineteenth century, outgrew its premises and moved to South Croydon, while the Whitgift Shopping Centre was built here on Whitgift Foundation Land. Following a period of research into the consumer and business needs of

Croydon, the centre was finished in 1968 and is now one of Britain's oldest shopping centres. These days every town has a shopping mall and they appear at times to be interchangeable, but Croydon does have the distinction of being at the forefront of the trend. In order to remain competitive and not appear as a relic from the 1960s building boom in Croydon, the Whitgift Centre underwent a huge refurbishment which was completed in 1995.

Flooding, Brighton Road, South Croydon, August 1937. A violent hour-long thunderstorm broke over South Croydon and Purley, resulting in scenes like this (see also page 80). There was a carpet of hail, and Croydon Airport was also very badly affected.

The Stag and Hounds pub, Selsdon Road, 1937. This photograph was taken (just before the pub was altered) by Mr T. Miller, who was the publican until 1966. The pub has a connection with Mr James Roffey, a well-respected gentleman of the district and also huntsman who ran the inn in the nineteenth century. It must have been well frequented because of its proximity to the cattle market.

CHAPTER FIVE

EAST CROYDON & ADDISCOMBE

Ashburton Park, 1960s. The model boating lake was filled in during the 1980s. Ashburton Park is on the site of Woodside Convent which now houses Ashburton Library. The park was the venue for Croydon Summer Show, a popular event for many years.

The NLA Tower and Harding and Co., Solicitors, Addiscombe Road, 1960s. East Bridge House, overshadowed here by the NLA Tower or 'Threepenny Bit Building', was home to Miss Kathleen Harding's firm of solicitors. For ten years she resisted all efforts to persuade her to sell her Edwardian house so the area could be developed, and finally agreed to leave in 1973, shortly before her lease expired. The house was finally demolished, but in the intermediate period the tower block was built and the new roundabout was carved out around her home.

East Croydon Station, looking east along Addiscombe Road, 1956. The Railway Hotel is on the right, but was demolished in the 1960s when the road was widened. Bridge House was built on the site and completed in 1983. The first East Croydon Station opened in 1841 and was rebuilt in 1894. The controversially designed new glass and steel structure which replaced the old station, opened in 1992.

Archbishop Tenison's School, *c.* 1891. The school was founded in North End in 1714 by Thomas Tenison, Archbishop of Canterbury, as a co-educational school for ten boys and ten girls, possibly the earliest mixed school in the country. It was rebuilt as separate girls' and boys' schools in Selsdon Road, South Croydon, in 1847. In 1930 the infants and juniors were transferred to other schools and the school reopened as a senior girls' school. It is now a mixed school once again in Selborne Road.

Park Hill Water Tower, *c.* 1950. Part of the small ornamental turret is missing here, having been damaged during the Second World War, although it was repaired at a later date. The watertower was erected in 1867 to improve the water supply to the higher areas of Croydon, such as the Park Hill Estate, which were developed at that time. It became a Grade II listed building in 1970 and has now been awarded a heritage plaque.

Oval House, Oval Road, 1974. Oval Road has an interesting history, which explains its particular shape. When the road was first developed six plots of land were for sale and there were no houses built. Potential house purchasers would have the right to use 'The Oval', or the central green 'as a pleasure ground'. However, less wealthy people moved into the area, a green in the middle was considered unnecessary and was therefore built upon.

The opening of the electric railway service, on the Mid Kent line at Addiscombe Station, 28 February 1926. Addiscombe Station was built in 1864, then rebuilt in brick in 1900. It was originally a terminus known as Croydon (Addiscombe Road) and Addiscombe (Croydon). It became known as Addiscombe from 1925. Passenger traffic was at its peak on this line during the 1930s, but by the 1980s only three through trains were running and the station was closed in May 1997. Part of the former rail route is to be used for Tramlink. The future of the station site is still undecided.

Bingham Halt, Lower Addsicombe Road, 1932. The two halts, Bingham Road and Spencer Road, which were wooden with 700-ft platforms, were closed in 1915 as part of the economies needed during the First World War and the local trains were not restored after this. In 1935 the station opened as Bingham Road and finally closed in 1983. Croydon Tramlink uses the old railway track here.

Bingham Road, site of St Mildred's Church, 1917. Plans were passed in 1931 for the present church and vicarage of St Mildred's at the junction of Sefton and Bingham Roads, and the new church was consecrated in 1932. There followed a new church hall in 1935 and the Museum, previously a wooden hut, was cased in brick and opened by Mr W.C. Berwick Sayers, Croydon's Chief Librarian.

The Black Horse Pub, Lower Addiscombe Road, 1960. The Black Horse probably dates back to the middle of the seventeenth century when it was a true village inn surrounded by fields with only a few cottages nearby. In the nineteenth century it was a popular haunt of the cadets from the nearby Addiscombe Military College. The building has undergone refurbishment to modernise this well-known local landmark.

Lower Addiscombe Road, looking east from the Black Horse Pub, 1953. Lower Addiscombe Road was known in the nineteenth century as St James' Road East, but usage has changed it to Lower Addiscombe Road as the ground level drops here. Addiscombe has always been a busy shopping area and there has been recent controversy over the decision to introduce parking restrictions along Lower Addiscombe Road.

CHAPTER SIX

NORWOOD & WOODSIDE

The old Sunnybank Bridge before it was replaced in 1959. A bus is having some difficulty manoeuvring round the corner. South Norwood suffered a great deal of bomb damage during the war years, and there was a particularly horrific incident in October 1944 when a V2 rocket fell behind the houses at Sunnybank, leaving six people dead and fourteen injured.

Upper Norwood recreation ground, *c.* 1938. Situated between Chevening Road and Eversley Road, Upper Norwood rec was acquired by the council in 1890 and opened by the Mayor, Councillor Frederick Edridge. He came directly to the ceremony from opening the new Wandle Park.

Spa Hill, 15 September 1926. This is the scene following an accident involving a car which ran amok, with fatal results, two people being killed and seven injured. The fencing of two houses was demolished and a lamp-post smashed. A newspaper report at the time stated the driver of the car was 'in a terrified state' and had mounted the pavement to avoid a dog as he was ascending Spa Hill in his vehicle.

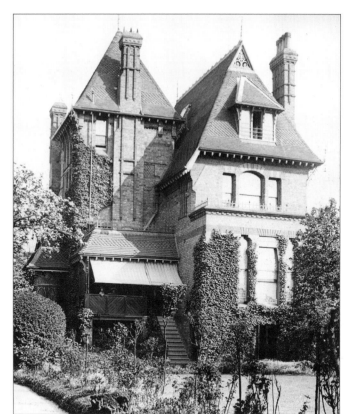

St Valery, Beulah Hill, *c.* 1900. This imposing Victorian Gothic-style house was built in 1880 by architect Sextus Dyball. It is a Grade II listed building which had been allowed to deteriorate in recent years, but has been saved from ruin by a Norwood Society campaign. It was converted into flats in 1996.

The Stanley Memorial Clock, top of Station Road, 1924. The Grade II listed clock was erected by the people of South Norwood to commemorate the golden wedding anniversary of the Stanleys in 1907. William Ford Robinson Stanley moved to South Norwood in 1867 with his family. He was a founder member of the Croydon Natural History and Scientific Society, and the inventor of tools and technical drawing and surveying equipment.

South Norwood High Street, *c.* 1935. The High Street is seen here in celebratory mood, possibly for King George V and Queen Mary's Silver Jubilee. The High Street area was developed along with the South Norwood Park and Selhurst Park Estates in the 1860s and 1870s. On the corner of Station Road is The Alliance Pub which dates from the mid-nineteenth century. It is believed the name commemorates the marriage between Edward VII, the Prince of Wales, and Princess Alexandra of Denmark. (*Reproduced by kind permission of the Croydon Advertiser Group.*)

Stanley Halls, South Norwood Hill, 1907. The Stanley Halls, which were Grade II listed in 1988, were built to Stanley's own designs for a community centre in 1902. There are two halls and an art gallery which was once home to Stanley's own collection of paintings. Stanley became a member of the Croydon School Board and built the Stanley Technical Trade School which still adjoins the Stanley Halls today. The halls have been used for local meetings and shows for almost a century, thanks to Stanley's generosity. A commemorative blue plaque is mounted outside the building.

Portland Road, South Norwood, from the railway bridge, 1953. The Portland Road area was first developed in the 1890s. Many of the early houses were built by local builders using local materials from the brick fields which once bordered the north-east side of Portland Road. Portland and Albert Roads were developed by R.L. Peacock and Son, of Station Road, who did so well they ended up living at the top of Manor Road in some luxury.

Portland Road and the Picture Palace Cinema, 1920. The first permanent cinema in South Norwood, the Central Hall Picture Palace was built in 1910. From the late 1930s it was known as the Central Cinema and was renamed the Rex in the 1950s. It closed in 1956 and for some years afterwards was known as the Portland Rooms offering facilities for wedding receptions and other functions. It is currently a furniture store.

South Norwood recreation ground, 1930. South Norwood rec was opened in 1889 and covers an area of 14 acres, with entrances in Selhurst, Tennison and Cargreen Roads. An early description of the ground claims 'seasonal lay-outs of flowers give it much charm and it is very popular'.

Woodside Green, 1961. In 1869 the Local Board of Health bought Woodside Green as an open space. A few years after this photograph was taken there were rumours that the green was to be developed. These came to nothing, but led to the formation of the Woodside Green Protection Society. There was originally a horse trough on the site of the War Memorial, but it was moved to where the green is intersected at the junction of Howard and Birchanger Roads.

CHAPTER SEVEN

SHIRLEY

St John the Evangelist Church, Shirley Church Road, 1959. The Grade II listed church was opened in 1856, having taken two years to build. Matthew Farrer became the first vicar of Shirley. In 1880 the Revd William Wilks (who grew the famous 'Shirley Poppy'), became vicar and instigated various changes both in the church and in the parish. These included music in church services, a parish magazine, clubs and the appointment of a village nurse.

Kenneth Baker, Secretary of State for Education, at building works at Shirley High School with the head teacher, Ian Russell in June 1986. Shirley Secondary Mixed School opened in Shirley Church Road in 1955, and was the first complete secondary school in the area.

Shirley Residential Schools' Band, early 1900s. The Shirley Schools were built in 1903 on the site of Shirley Lodge Farm in Wickham Road. The schools were founded for the 'board, education and training' of Bermondsey Poor Law children. The community lived in thirty-seven self-contained cottages, each named after plants or flowers. In the 1920s the schools were taken over by the London County Council. In 1970 the decision was taken to demolish the schools and work began on the estate known as Shirley Oaks Village in 1984.

Wickham Road, north side, 1959. This block of shops and flats was designed by architect Donald Rowswell and built in 1958. Wickham Road at one time linked the villages of Shirley and Wickham. Until the building boom of the 1930s Shirley was a small village, with the main housing area being Upper Shirley Road, along Wickham Road and between Shirley Road and Spring Park Road. Some shops began to appear in Wickham Road, which was widened to take the subsequent increase in traffic.

The Glade, Monks Orchard, looking north from where Greenview Avenue was later built on the right, 1923. First mentioned in local records in 1511, The Glade and the adjoining fields were formerly part of Ham Farm. This area was developed from the early 1920s, although the early roads followed existing farm tracks and building took place in a haphazard manner.

Shirley Afternoon Townswomen's Guild 21st birthday party, 4 June 1965. The ladies were dancing 'The Gay Gordons'. At the very first meeting in 1944, members were forced to duck under tables as a doodlebug bomb flew overhead, and the following year the house where the meetings were held was completely destroyed. Today the Guild meets in the Shirley Parish Hall in Wickham Road and continues to have an enthusiastic membership.

The Sandrock Hotel, Upper Shirley Road, looking down Sandpits Road, 1960. The Sandrock Hotel was built in 1867 in actual sandpits, the local industry of sand-digging being a flourishing concern. The disorderly behaviour of visitors to the recently opened public space of Shirley and Addington Hills in 1879 caused The Sandrock to lose its Sunday licence for some years until peace could once more reign unchallenged!

Shirley Fountain, opposite the Sandrock Hotel, 1906. The drinking fountain was known as the Farrer Memorial, named after Matthew Farrer (see page 53). When built in 1880 it was a pump, but was converted to a drinking fountain in 1890 when mains water was brought to the cottages opposite the Sandrock Pub. The fountain fell into disrepair and was removed in the late 1960s. There is a commemorative seat on the site.

Spring Park Wood, c. 1926. Spring Park Wood is a small area of woodland shown here before Links View Road was extended to Bridle Road. Although concealed behind houses on all sides, it supports a wide range of flora and fauna.

The Shirley Park Hotel, showing the south and east fronts, January 1960. The Shirley Park Hotel started life in 1649 as Shirley House on the east side of Shirley Road. It was rebuilt between 1720 and 1721 by John Claxton to a 'substantial and commodious design of his own'. Its name was changed briefly to Shirley Hall from 1895 until 1901 and in 1913 it became a hotel. Falling profits and the popular trend at the time for new buildings, rather than the unfashionable structures of old, sadly led to its demolition in 1962. Trinity School now occupies the site.

Shirley Parade, Shirley Road, 1947. The row of fourteen shops was built by the now busy roundabout in 1928. Shirley Road was first known as Stroud Green Lane, but its name was changed following a petition by residents who complained that their post was going to a Stroud Green in North London.

CHAPTER EIGHT
ADDINGTON

Farming at Homestead Way, 1947. The name Homestead came from a field shown on the Tithe Map, Homestead Pasture. The road was laid out in 1949 as part of the post-war development of New Addington.

Addington Hills, Bridle Path,
c. 1900. Addington Hills still looks
very rural in appearance today. It is
the largest public open space in
Croydon. Addington parish was
merged with the then County Borough
of Croydon in 1927.

The Valve House, Addington Hills, 1906. This building housed the valves for the Addington
Reservoir, and Tea Rooms serving refreshments were on the ground floor. It was demolished after
the typhoid fever outbreak of 1937, which was traced to the reservoir. Addington Well was found
to be too heavily polluted for the public water supply.

Addington Forge, 1909. The earliest records of the Addington Forge building date from around 1740, when it was built on the site of an earlier burnt-out forge/smithy. A new forge was completely reconstructed in 1815. The forge was worked by members of the Coppin family for many years and the business continued to thrive well into the twentieth century. Although horses are no longer shod there, the Forge is now home to a long established ornamental ironwork business run by the Collins family.

Ballards Farm Estate, *c.* 1938. Costains had been building new developments in the area since 1925 and this particular house was constructed in the style of those in the popular Disney film *Snow White and the Seven Dwarfs*. The whole of the Ballards estate, which ran to Selsdon Park Road and included Ballards Farm and Heathfield, belonged to Charles Goschen until 1915 when the estate was put up for sale. Heathfield House was bought by Alderman H. Houlder, Mayor of Croydon. Mr Hollingsworth, of Bourne and Hollingsworth department store fame, bought Ballards Mansion and grounds which he gave to the Wholesale Drapers' & Clerks' School at Russell Hill, Purley. A new building was erected and the school moved to their new premises, now known as Royal Russell School (see page 121).

The Lion Lodge and Gates to Addington Palace, Spout Hill, 1960. In 1771 Robert Mylne was appointed as architect for the first house, which was later to become Addington Palace, home to six archbishops as their occasional residence. The archbishops made great changes to the buildings to accommodate their needs. Mylne built the Lion Lodges halfway up Spout Hill, moving the gate pillars from the western side of the old mansion to their new position. They are now private residences.

Addington Palace with the Great Cedar of Lebanon in the foreground. The Great Cedar in the grounds of Addington Palace was thought to have been planted in the late eighteenth century at about the time Capability Brown was landscaping the grounds. It is said to be one of the largest cedars in the British Isles and has been awarded a commemorative plaque as one of the 'great trees of London'.

Castle Hill Cottages, pre-1955. The cottages were built in 1889/90. Castle Hill is traditionally linked with the legendary castle of Baron Robert Aguillon who lived in Addington in the thirteenth century. Castle Hill Farm stood at the corner of Lodge Lane and Headley Drive and took its name from the hillside on which it stood. The farmhouse was demolished in about 1955, and the cottages with it.

A fire at St George's Church Hall, March 1958. St George's Hall was New Addington's first church building and was consecrated in 1947 when it was a converted army hut. It was destroyed by fire in mysterious circumstances in March 1958. A new church hall for the Castle Hill area was built in 1963.

An aerial view of the New Addington factory estate, early 1950s. All of the industry for the New Addington area has been concentrated around the factory estate in King Henry's Drive, centred around Vulcan Way. The first factory was built in 1950 to provide local employment and more were opened in 1951. However, plans to extend the industrial area eastward onto land belonging to Bromley Council were blocked and no further development took place.

The opening of New Addington Market, Central Parade, 1973. The idea of an open-air market to be sited on the area just in front of the shops in Central Parade was first considered in 1972. The market opened in June of the following year on Tuesdays and Fridays, although it takes place only on Fridays now. It continues to flourish, being extremely well supported by local residents.

CHAPTER NINE

SELSDON &
SANDERSTEAD

*Hamsey Green Pond, looking south-west across Limpsfield Road, 1961. The pond is situated
on the corner of Limpsfield Road and Kingswood Lane, almost at the borough boundary.
It disappeared for many years, having been silted up, but was restored in the 1970s when
new vegetation was introduced.*

Hubbard and Nash's Shop, 145 Addington Road, Selsdon, 1936. The hardware shop is pictured fairly soon after its opening in 1934. It is still in business today, in the block of shops known as The Broadway which were built in 1925 by Costains who developed the huge estate at Selsdon.

Royal British Legion Parade, Addington Road, Selsdon, 24 May 1957. The British Legion was particularly active at this time, as its members included many veterans of both World Wars. Addington Road was widened during the 1930s to accommodate increasing traffic levels and in 1968 traffic lights were installed at the junction of Addington Road/Farley Road to help ease the congestion.

The opening of The Good Neighbour inn, Addington Road, Selsdon, 20 September 1956. The Good Neighbour changed its name to The Stag in 1983 and was refurbished, with changes including the fitting out of a family room and the opening of a beer garden

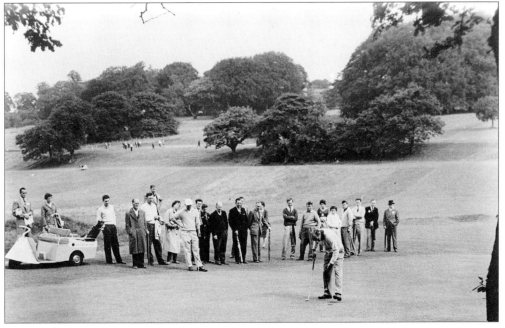

The Sprite Tournament, Selsdon Park Golf Club, 1960. Alan Doble Sanderson acquired Selsdon Park in 1924 and converted the house into a hotel. He developed a full-size golf course in the 200-acre grounds, which opened in 1929. The course was laid out by J.H. Taylor, who also designed the course at Purley Downs. The club was closed to the public after 1986 and reverted to the sole use of the hotel guests (see page 68).

Highland cattle in a lowland setting at Selsdon Park, early 1900s. The last private owner of Selsdon Park was Wickham Noakes, a country gentleman who bought the estate in 1899 and lived there until his death in 1923. He purchased the estate so he could continue his sporting pursuits, and entertained hunting friends and business associates there (see page 67).

Purley Oaks Road, junction with Downsway, looking east, May 1954. Purley Oaks Road was developed in 1903 and named after the ancient oak trees which surrounded Purley Oaks Farm. The coat of arms of Coulsdon and Purley Urban District Council features a shield decorated with two trees, which represent Purley Oaks and Purley Beeches.

View of Sanderstead, looking towards Hurst View Road, 1936, photographed from the rear of Lismore Road. In 1928 housing development was taking place, Croham Close, Hurst View Road and Hurst Way were built and Croham Manor Road was extended to Selsdon Road over the former footpath. Until this time Croham Manor had finished at Croham Hurst Woods.

Sanderstead Horticultural Society Flower Show at Sanderstead Congregational church hall, July 1954. Sanderstead Congregational church dates from 1933. The buildings, including the hall, were completed in May 1933 and in 1972 the church became the United Reformed church. Sanderstead Horticultural Society originated from a wartime 'Dig For Victory' show in 1941 and continues to have a large, committed membership after nearly sixty years.

The demolition of St Anne's College, Sanderstead Road, November 1981. St Anne's College was opened in 1909 by the Catholic Convent of the Ladies of Mary, who also opened Coloma Convent School in 1869. In the 1970s limited space made it impossible for the school to expand, so in 1977 St Anne's College became part of Coloma School and the girls moved to the Coloma site in Upper Shirley Road.

Sanderstead Pond with All Saints' Church in the background to the left and the new church hall in the middle background, 1961. The pond is at 'The Gruffy' – the green, open, space which surrounds the pond – and this and Grade I-listed All Saints' Church are the main reminders of the former medieval village here.

CHAPTER TEN

COULSDON, PURLEY & KENLEY

Harvesting at Coulsdon North Estate, looking towards Stoats Nest Village, August 1954.
Stoats Nest Village was named after the farm which stood on the corner of Brighton Road.
The farmland was developed for building in the 1960s.

The Red Lion pub, before 1927 when it was rebuilt. The Red Lion has occupied its present site on the Brighton Road, at Smitham Bottom (now Coulsdon), since at least the seventeenth century. It became an important coaching inn on the London to Brighton route in the nineteenth century.

Purley Chamber of Commerce Dinner at the Red Lion pub, Coulsdon, 30 November 1954. Purley's business group closed in the 1980s due to a lack of members. Since the Chamber folded Purley has come under the umbrella of Croydon and South London Chamber of Commerce. In the last few years traders have been asked whether they wanted to reform the Chamber in order to help boost Purley's image and halt the trend for closure of local shops.

The Skew Bridge, near Coulsdon South Station, 1954. The bridge takes the fast line or 'Quarry Line' over the main Brighton Road. The line is seen here entering the covered section in the grounds of Cane Hill Hospital and the men in the lower picture are dismantling its cover later in the same year .The 'Quarry Line' was built in 1897/9 as a result of the conflict between the South Eastern Railway Co. and the London, Brighton and South Coast Railway Co. who both had running rights over the original line. South of Coulsdon the 'Quarry Line' crosses the Brighton Road on iron girder bridges.

The last train leaves Coulsdon North Station, 30 September 1983. A crowd gathered to wave off the train which was actually five minutes late when it arrived! Coulsdon North Station, which opened in 1899, had a series of name changes, originally being called Stoats Nest. A previous Stoats Nest Station had closed to passenger traffic in 1856. In 1911 it was renamed Coulsdon and Smitham Downs for Cane Hill, later Coulsdon West and, finally, Coulsdon North. When the station closed in 1983 as a result of British Rail's rationalisation of services, train services were transferred to the nearby Smitham Station. Below, model railway enthusiasts can be seen at an exhibition at Cousldon North Station in March 1954.

Dog training at the Scouts Hut, Coulsdon South Station, March 1954. The canine pupils being put through their paces here belonged to members of the Coulsdon Branch of the Associated Sheep, Police and Army Dogs' Society. Although there is no longer such a specialised club in existence, Purley and Coulsdon still have a Dog Training Society.

Farewell party in January 1961 for the Revd M.B. Segal, Priest-in-charge of St Francis' Church, Rickman Hill, 1953–61. The Ven P.D. Robb, Vicar of St Andrew's Church, is on the left and the handbell ringers are from Croydon Parish Church. St Francis' Church was sold in April 1989 and is now the Coptic Orthodox Church of St Mary and St Shenouda.

St Andrew's Church, Coulsdon, April 1950. The church, seen here after an unseasonal fall of snow, is at the junction of Woodcote Grove Road and Woodmansterne Road. The foundation stone of the present building was laid in April 1914 but the construction of the church was not fully completed until 1964, just in time for its Golden Jubilee.

Coulsdon Working Men's Club cricket team, Marlpit Lane recreation ground, 1930. The photograph was supplied by Bill Purver who was captain: he is the team member seated second from the left in the back row. The club was in Victoria Road, Coulsdon.

Hall and Co.'s Lime Works, Marlpit Lane, 1961. The chalk quarries and limeworks which belonged to Hall Bros (established in 1824) began operating in 1864. They provided the lime used for the company's cement works. The Marlpit Quarry floor is now covered by the Ullswater Industrial Estate where Hall and Co. Builders' Merchants still have a depot. At one time Hall and Co. had premises at Victoria Wharf, Cherry Orchard Road and their output of white lime 'far exceeded that of any other works in the South of England'.

Bradmore Farm and the barn to the right, Bradmore Green, August 1954. The little boy is showing blatant disregard for the 'No Paddling' notice! Bradmore Green pond was once a vital water source for villagers and their livestock. A number of ponds in the area were dug and maintained, using money from charities set up by local benefactors. The barn was probably the original farmhouse, as parts of it date back to the sixteenth century. The present farmhouse is for the most part an eighteenth-century building.

Mrs Hollands' shop, General Stores and Post Office, 210 Coulsdon Road, May 1932. The half-timbered house at 210 Coulsdon Road is known as Cherry Tree Cottage. It has had a number of uses apart from being a private home; it was once a public house, a cricket club headquarters and a butcher's shop. It was known as a 'general shop' from 1924 until at least 1939 and would have played a vital part in village life, being the post office and containing the fire alarm and ambulance telephone.

Gardner's Tea Gardens, Godstone Road, entrance and façade, 1913. William Gardner's Pleasure Resort, Temperance Hotel and Tea Gardens became very popular with visitors on day trips from London and as a suitable venue for Sunday School outings. Among the attractions were a narrow-gauge railway, a small zoo, donkey rides, swings and roundabouts. Gardner's Tea Rooms closed down in the 1930s, although the house itself still stands and is marked with a Bourne Society plaque.

Two views of Bank Holiday scenes in Purley, almost 50 years apart. Above, the crowds are waiting for the tram, *c.* 1911. Trams reached Purley when the service was electrified in 1901/2. In 1902 a crossover line was installed at Purley Corner which became known as Purley Tram Terminus. During Edwardian times trams were very popular, taking visitors to within walking distance of attractions like Gardner's Tea Rooms. In the scene below, in August 1958, the car has taken the place of the tram, the traffic is approaching Purley Corner or Cross and an enterprising boy is selling newspapers to the returning day trippers stuck in the queue.

The congregation of St Mark's Church, Church Road, Purley, present a car to the Revd E.A. Shattock, 1932. The foundation stone of Grade II listed St Mark's Church was laid in 1909, although earlier in 1905 a 'tin hut' was built as a temporary chapel for St Mark's in Peaks Hill Ridge (now Church Road) which was only to be used for five years. In fact it was used as a church hall for a further fifty-seven years.

Flooding and hail in Purley Road, 30 August 1937. A freak storm hit north Surrey, and South Croydon, Purley and Coulsdon were badly affected by the sudden and dramatic flooding which occurred. A report in *The Coulsdon & Purley Weekly Record* says: 'the water was over two feet deep at South Croydon and Purley pavements and front gardens could not be seen for water . . . shopkeepers fought a brave battle against the water with brooms' (see page 40).

The River Bourne floods at Brighton Road, Purley, February 1928. This was the site of the Imperial Ice Rink which opened on 5 February 1931, according to *The Purley Review*, and was the largest in Europe. It was a successful venue for nearly twenty years, but when the pipes used for freezing needed to be replaced after the war, the cost of steel was found to be prohibitive and the rink closed in May 1950. It became the Orchid Ballroom. A sewer relief scheme implemented in the 1960s brought an end to the worst of the flooding episodes.

Purley Bury House, showing the original front of the building, now the rear, 1954. Purley Bury House, which is situated in a cul-de-sac, Lexington Court, off Purley Bury Avenue, is the only really old building in Purley. It dates from the reign of Elizabeth 1 when it was occupied by Sir Thomas Saunders, Remembrancer of the Exchequer. It was subsequently inhabited by the Kings, the Greshams, the Attwoods and the Hawtreys. For many years it was used as a nursing home and recently a number of terraced houses have been constructed from the part of the house that adjoined the conservatory.

Garston Hall, Kenley, from Old Lodge Lane, May 1939. Garston Hall, which once dominated the hamlet of Wattenden, is known to have existed as long ago as 1269. It was marked on Rocque's Map of Surrey of 1768, but spelt Garsdon. The house was damaged during the Second World War and demolished in 1945 for safety reasons.

Godstone Road near the Kenley Hotel, 1947. The Kenley Hotel dates from around 1869 and the station at its rear opened in 1856. Kenley was part of Coulsdon Manor which covered the whole area known as Coulsdon, Old Coulsdon, Purley and Kenley. Kenley was primarily farm land until the mid-nineteenth century, when large properties began to appear south of Godstone Road, and it was created a parish in its own right in 1888. The area still has a rural air to it today, with Riddlesdown to the north of Godstone Road and Kenley Common to the south.

RAF Kenley firefighting display, 1954. Kenley Aerodrome opened during the First World War and played an important part in the Battle of Britain as RAF Kenley. After the war Kenley was in use only as an RAF Headquarters Unit and in recent years the only regular flying to take place is in gliders by members of the local gliding club and the Air Training Corps.

Miss L. Hall opens Betts Mead Recreation Ground, Kenley, July 1925. Betts Mead, between Old Lodge Lane and Hayes Lane, was acquired by Coulsdon and Purley Urban District Council over a number of years. The first portion of land was given to the council by Frederick Betts Esq., who presented it 'for the perpetual use of the public for a recreation ground and park'.

CHAPTER ELEVEN

WARTIME

*A Royal Enfield motorcycles outing for wounded soldiers, Parchmore Road, July 1916.
Wounded soldiers from Croydon hospitals would often spend their leave at Whitehorne
Cottage, a seventeenth-century building which stood in Thornton Road and was also used
as an air raid shelter.*

Ingram Road War Hospital, March 1917. As part of the war effort public and private buildings were converted into military hospitals, and in Croydon six schools were used: Ingram Road (see page 95), Davidson, Ecclesbourne and Stanford Roads, and The Crescent Boys' and Girls' Schools. The first patients were admitted in June 1915 and the hospitals closed in May 1919.

Mr Geoff Rollason wearing the Whitgift School Officer Training Corps (OTC) uniform, 1926. The uniform consisted of a peaked hat, jacket, breeches to the knee and puttees. After the war it was called the Combined Cadet Corps. The young men were being trained as navy and air cadets.

Waste paper collection, 1939/45.
A salvage campaign ran throughout
the war in which food, clothes, metals,
etc., were recycled: everything which
could be, was reused! The people in
the picture are giving books for
pulping. Every house in the borough
was provided with a sack in which to
put waste paper, and the dustcarts
were equipped with trailers into which
the sacks could be emptied.

Coulsdon and Purley UDC salvage exhibition, 1941. Waste food collection and processing began in the early 1940s and everyone who was able to was encouraged to produce food. Neighbours formed pig clubs and waste food bins were sited all around Croydon to take scraps which could be fed to the animals.

59th Surrey (Addington Battalion) Home Guard, *c.* 1943. The weapon around which the Home Guard and interested youngsters are clustered was called a spigot mortar. These were issued to Home Guard battalions in 1943, so this scene must be during the second half of the war. The bomb with which the crew have loaded the weapon has the word 'SAND' printed across it. Instead of high explosive, the inert rounds used for practice were filled with sand.

Bird scaring on the wheatfields, Purley Way, 1943. As supplies of food from Europe were cut and rationing tightened its grip, farmers switched from growing vegetables to cultivating corn for bread and other crops for animal feed. The nation was encouraged to 'Dig For Victory' and any suitable spare piece of ground, lawns, flowerbeds, etc., was turned over to vegetable production.

ARP Wardens at Woodside School, 1939/45. Jack Steel is third from the left in the second row and George Steel, who ran the family greengrocers' business, is in the back row, third from the right. Air Raid Precautions Wardens were recruited from 1935 onwards and played a vital part in the Civil Defence campaign during the Second World War. The majority of the members of the warden service were volunteers. Their duties were wide ranging, and they were often the first to brave the debris of dangerous buildings and bring out casualties. They played an equally important role in helping to keep up people's spirits during the long hours spent in the air raid shelters (see page 110).

A Christmas party at Mayday Hospital Wartime Nursery, 1939/45. The toys and Father Christmas which were supplied by Kennards of Croydon do not seem to have brought smiles to most of these children's faces, although no doubt the nurses were doing their best to give them a happy few hours in those troubled times.

Thanksgiving Parade For Victory In Europe, Katharine Street, Sunday 13 May 1945. The Victory Parade was part of the celebrations in Croydon to mark the end of the war in Europe. There was a mile-long procession, leading to an assembly at the Town Hall for the service. Representatives from all sections of the national and local war effort took part.

CHAPTER TWELVE

EDUCATION

John Fisher School Sports, May 1954. The Roman Catholic boys' school was formerly at
Duppas Hill but was moved to its current premises in Peaks Hill in 1931. The school is
maintained by the London Borough of Sutton, but takes boys from Croydon too.

The opening of the new Woodcote Secondary School, Meadow Rise, July 1957. Shown here are Mr J.C. Thompson, Alderman C. Black and the head, K.R. Johns. The school was founded in 1905 as Smitham Bottom Council Mixed School in Chipstead Valley Road. During the Second World War large numbers of pupils were evacuated and at one stage only three working classes were left in the school. Numbers soon recovered after the war when the school was known as Smitham County (Mixed) School, and from 1972 it became a comprehensive school which it remains.

Addington National School, Addington Village Road, 1930. In 1794 the site of the village school at the foot of Spout Hill was occupied by two cottages which were known as the Workhouse. The cottages had been converted into a workhouse/school and in 1820 the school was affiliated to the National Society for the Education of the Poor when it became known as the 'Addington National School'. The cottages were demolished in 1844 and a new school erected by Archbishop William Howley. This school continued until 1950 and then the building served as a village hall until it was finally demolished in 1967.

Founders Day at Coloma School, Tavistock Road, June 1923. Pictured are the Mayor and Mayoress of Croydon, Mr and Mrs T.W. Wood-Roberts. An article in the school magazine at the time says 'an interesting feature of the afternoon were the "Country Dances" performed in the open' and the event was obviously a success, as by 8pm stalls which had been set out looked 'in a sad plight'.

The Homestead Preparatory School section of Croydon High School, 1965. The Homestead stood on the site of Lunar House in Wellesley Road. Croydon High School was founded in 1874 and occupied the Wellesley Road site until 1880 when it moved to the present buildings in Old Farleigh Road, Selsdon, where it remained until 1966. The Homestead was for seven to eleven year olds and there was also was another building for infants, The Elms.

Whitgift School, porter's lodge, c. 1900. Whitgift School opened in 1871 in North End. The porter's lodge was built in a red brickwork Perpendicular-Gothic style, corresponding with that of the other school buildings which were erected at a cost of about £14,000 on the Whitgift Centre site. The buildings were demolished in 1965 to make way for the Whitgift Centre (see pages 38–9, 121).

Harvest Festival at Waddon Junior School, 1950. Mrs Betty Smith (née Cusden) is standing second right, immediately behind the seated children. Waddon Infant and Junior Schools were combined from 1934 until 1952 when the nearby Duppas Infant and Junior School was reorganised as a junior school and Waddon Infant and Junior School became a school for infants only.

Ingram Infants' School, Class II a, 1931. Mrs Eileen Baker (*née* Holman) is seated on the right in the second row on the inside. Miss Kath Frost is seated two rows behind her on the right. Miss Kate M. Baker was the headmistress from 1919 until 1942 when she retired. The school opened in May 1905, there were separate boys' and girls' schools on the same site and, in 1932, schools were organised for senior boys, senior girls and infants. The school has now become David Livingstone Primary in Northwood Road, Thornton Heath.

Mr J.D. Davies, head of Thornton Heath Private Boys' School from 1902 until 1937/8. Mr Davies is shown here with his wife Winifred and daughter Joy (1916–71) (see page 96).

Prize-giving at Thornton Heath School Annual Sports, in the 1920s. The annual sports were held at Barclays Bank Ground, London Road, Norbury. Many of the trophies were bought by the head, Mr J.D. Davies, and the event was always held on a Wednesday which was traditionally 'half day'. Thornton Heath School was founded in 1884 by Mr A.C. Dent; in 1888 it was moved to Beaumont House in Quadrant Road as larger premises were required. The school had many locations: from 1915 until 1928 it was at The Grove (later 933 London Road), and from 1928 until 1935 at Silverleigh at the junction of Grove and Goldcrest Roads. For the last years, until it closed in 1939, it was at 167 Brigstock Road (see page 95).

CHAPTER THIRTEEN

TRANSPORT

*A stretch of track at the Woodside to Elmers End railway, early 1930s. The golf range is
to the right; this is the site of one of the Tramlink junctions.*

The *Brighton Belle* (1100 hours from Victoria Station) on the fast line approaching Woodplace Lane Bridge, Coulsdon, on the last day of scheduled service, Sunday 30 April 1972. The London Victoria to Brighton service known as the 'Pullman Brighton Belle' became famous for its theatrical clientele, including Dame Flora Robson and Lord Olivier. There were a large number of West End performers who commuted daily, as the timing of the service suited the hours of those working in the theatre.

An open-top tram at West Croydon Station, early 1930s. The last day of open-top trams in service on the West Croydon to Crystal Palace route was 8 February 1936. The following day the trolleybus service commenced the Crystal Palace run (see page 103).

The last tram, April 1951. When the last tram left Purley depot in April 1951 a considerable crowd assembled and all along the Brighton Road people lined the route, although it was pouring with rain, to witness its final journey. Trams are soon to run in Croydon once again. The 1991 Croydon Tramlink Bill received Royal Assent in July 1994 and the new tram route will run around central Croydon and out to New Addington, Wimbledon and Beckenham.

Purley depot, 1951. Croydon Tramways began a service which ran between Norbury and Purley in 1901. A tram depot had been built on the Brighton Road at the bottom of Purley Downs Road and was extended in 1907 to hold up to thirty-six trams. The depot was later used as the Texas do-it-yourself store in 1984, but was demolished in 1992.

The laying of tramlines in the 1930s. Croydon and South Metropolitan Tramways became part of the London Passenger Transport Board (London Transport as we know it today) in 1933 and there followed route changes, closures and conversions to trolleybus operation. Twenty-five years after the last trolleybus route closed Croydon was identified as a potential area for light railway development and proposals for Croydon Tramlink, due to be operational by the year 2000, followed.

The pedestrianisation of North End, September 1990. Below, an old original tramline is being unearthed during the works in North End. Almost half a century after their demise trams are to run around the area for the second time and it is to be hoped the new environmentally friendly trams won't add to existing traffic congestion, but will help to ease the problem.

Lendon Bros, car firm at a rally, South Norwood Recreation Ground, late 1930s/early 1940s. The family business, which started in 1925 in South Norwood and moved to Coulsdon in 1978, closed in 1992 laying off thirty staff.

Reeves Motor Hire Co. at Whytecliffe Road North, Purley, c. 1905. Levison Reeves, who started up the firm in 1896, is standing to the right of the car at the front. The business, whose motto was 'Good Service', failed in the slump between the wars in 1928 (see page 106).

South Croydon Bus Garage, *c.* 1925. South Croydon garage was built by Tillings in 1915. This interior of the garage shows a line-up of buses operating on routes 12A, 34, 75A and 159A. Tilling's transport business was founded in 1847 by Thomas Tilling when he first bought a horse and carriage for hiring purposes, and was an important name in motor passenger transport in London for seventy years.

South Croydon Bus Garage, March 1957. An RT type bus, number 2052, is changing crews outside its home base while working (Sundays only) route 59, which went from West Hampstead to Chipstead Valley.

Trolleybus 491 on route 654 at the foot of Anerley Hill, 28 February 1959. A special problem which arose on the Croydon–Crystal Palace section was that of ensuring safety on Anerley Hill, which rises sharply to the Palace, and all trolleybuses were fitted with run back brakes. The final day of operation on trolleybus route 654 was the following Wednesday, 4 March. It was then replaced by new motor bus route 154 and routes 157 and 64 were extended (see page 98).

Barclay Road bus stand, August 1955. The first day of the 'Express' service on route 130, RT type bus number 3111 of South Croydon Garage (nearest the stop) and, behind it route 119, RT type bus number 173 of Bromley Garage. The conductor is displaying his Bell Punch ticket punch and is wearing the white summer top on his cap; the driver is also wearing a white summer uniform coat.

A Bourne and Balmer coach party, *c.* 1930. Bourne and Balmer Ltd, who were known as Croydon's leading firm of coach operators, started as a removal company in George Street in 1924. They ran an excursion fleet to the coast before the Second World War. The firm was later acquired by A.Timpson & Sons Ltd of Catford, who themselves became part of the National Travel organisation.

Skinner's of Croydon chain drive Commer van, *c.* 1930. The firm of A.G. Skinner was established in 1923, and Alfred Gladstone Skinner, removal contractor, operated from his home at 10 Upper Coombe Street, Croydon. He moved to premises in South End in 1928, where they had warehouse facilities too. The business closed in 1979.

CHAPTER FOURTEEN

PEOPLE AT WORK

*W.H. Polhill & Sons, 1903–15. Polhill and Sons were pork butchers in North End, who also
had premises in Church Street and South End. They continued in business until 1927.*

Reeves Garage, High Street, Purley, *c.* 1910. Levison Reeves, who owned the company, is to the left wearing a hat, Arthur Reeves is astride the bike and Molly Reeves is the little girl standing in the foreground. The family lived at 36 Brighton Road, Purley. Levison became the maintenance manager for Costains the builders and then started a building company based in Tatsfield. The garage was then taken over by George Reeves (see page 101).

The firm of Hardstone, Isted and Pursley, annual outing to Brighton, 1935/6. Mr George Hardstone is standing on the left. The firm of decorators are pictured opposite the Conservative Club in St Peter's Road, South Croydon. George Hardstone and A. Isted and Sons were in existence until 1974.

Two views of the firm of Cusdens, of South Croydon. Above, the firm of E.G. Cusden, builders and ironmongers, in its premises at 19 Croham Road in the 1930s. The business continued until 1957. Mr E.G. Cusden is on the right, Mr E.A. Cusden (his son) is in the doorway. The premises are still there and are now home to a florist. The lower scene is of E.A. Cusden's building firm's outing in 1954. The firm was established in 1944 and is still in existence in Croham Road.

The first mechanised delivery service at Nobles the chemist, Selsdon Road, *c.* 1907. Sam Noble at The Imperial Pharmacy, 12 Ye Market Place, Selsdon Road, specialised in homeopathic remedies in the early years of this century, long before they became widely accepted as part of mainstream medicine. Mr Noble has another claim to fame, in that his was the chemist shop where weedkiller containing arsenic was bought to be used in the notorious Birdhurst Poisonings of the late 1920s.

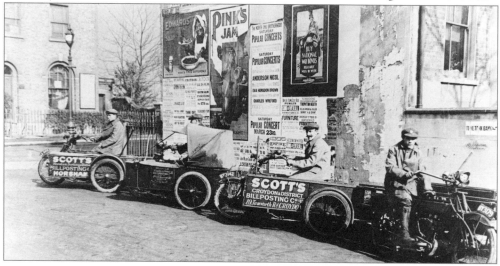

Scotts Bill Posting Company, Keeley Road/Tamworth Road junction, 1918. The firm of Alexander Scott's Poster Service Ltd was established in 1741 when Mr Scott of Lambeth advertised himself as 'The Champion Billposter'. One of his successors, another Mr A. Scott, began to use Enfield motorcycles and sidecars instead of horses, carts and handbarrows, following the loss of most of his workforce with the onset of the First World War. This enabled him to carry out the same amount of work with fewer men. The firm moved to Whitehorse Road in 1959, but were no longer in business there after 1968.

R. Mansell, builders, constructing four shops, Croydon High Street, 1928. The photograph is from the collection of Harry Albert Holloway, who was a foreman at Mansell's. The business was founded in 1908 in Grant Road, Addiscombe, and their headquarters is still on the same site, at Roman House.

Hellings' dairy firm delivering milk at Duppas Hill, *c.* 1903. F. Hellings' Central Dairy was established in Queen Street in the mid-nineteenth century and also had 'handsome new premises' at 1 Grand Parade, High Street, Croydon from 1897 until 1928. In 1929 the Express Dairy Co. took over the premises.

G.W. Steel's greengrocers' shop, Woodside Green, early twentieth century. The boy holding the horse is Frank Steel and his brother G.W. Steel is outside the shop, behind the cart. The building was condemned during the the First World War, so the business moved to 16 Stroud Road, where it remained until closure in 1977. The original building, however, stood on Woodside Green until 1987 (see page 89).

John Jakson's peppermint distillery, Mitcham Road, in the 1930s. Mitcham and its environs became famous in the nineteenth century for the production of high quality lavender and peppermint oils. By the 1880s the largest producer was John Jakson's distillery in Mitcham Road, which stood on the site where Challenge House is today. The company was thriving until the 1930s, when the farmland around the distillery was sold for development, and after the war the company wound down.

CHAPTER FIFTEEN

ENTERTAINMENT & LEISURE

Guide Camp, c. 1927. Ivy Wilkinson from South Croydon is flanked by fellow Girl Guides, enjoying themselves in the West Country. Both Ivy and her sister Elsie enjoyed Brownies and Guides in Croydon.

Brownies, 1948. Mrs Corinne Wilson (*née* Searle) is in the centre of the middle row. The Brownie Pack meetings were held at George Street Congregational Church which stood in George Street West from 1878 until 1962, when it was demolished to allow for new developments of shops and offices. The new church in Addiscombe Grove was opened in March 1964 and is now known as East Croydon United Reformed Church.

Guides' pageant, Marlpit Lane recreation ground, May 1957. We know the rec as Coulsdon Memorial Ground today. A pageant of 'Guiding through the ages' was presented by Coulsdon District Girl Guides, comprising six companies, as part of the local Guide celebrations to mark the centenary of the birth of Lord Baden-Powell. The girls are wearing the large floppy hats of Guides during the First World War. A newspaper report of the time says 'it was a cold and windy evening' and the girls were told to wear extra woollies.

The Cinematograph Theatre, North End, 1915. The Croydon Cinematograph Theatre/Palladium was opened in December 1910 as the eleventh cinema built in the London area for the Pyke Circuit, whose director was Montagu Pyke. The Pyke Circuit ran into financial difficulties and new management took over in 1915 and renamed the cinema the Palladium. It closed in May 1930, having been bought by Woolworth's which still stands on the site with the original frontage above ground floor level little altered.

The Pembroke Theatre, Wellesley Road, 1961. The Pembroke Theatre, which opened as the Pembroke Hall in 1897, had the distinction of being Britain's first permanent 'Theatre In the Round'. The building took its name from Croydon's MP from 1886 to 1895, the Hon. Sidney Herbert who became the Earl of Pembroke. The theatre closed in 1962 following a record attendance at the last ever performance of the play *The Summer People*.

Nativity Scene at the Missionary Pageant, Croydon, Christmas 1929. There were a number of mission halls around at this time including London City Mission Halls in Gloucester Road, Cairo Road, Gillett Road and Portland Road.

Roy Hudd, facing us on the right, jiving at the Orchid Ballroom, Purley, November 1955. For many years, following its opening in 1950, the Orchid Ballroom was a popular venue for dancing and there is still an entertainment venue on the site today.

Purley Way pool, 1930s. Purley Way open-air swimming pool opened in 1935 and proved to be very popular in the early days. It closed in 1979 as it was in need of major repairs and falling attendances were blamed on indifferent British weather. The often chilly summer temperatures were failing to heat the water.

St Luke's, Woodside Football Club, 1916/17. In June 1929 St Luke's team was admitted to the Excelsior League and an entry in the *Woodside Parish Magazine* reads: 'We must congratulate the club on its entry into league football and wish it every success during the coming season'.

St George's Day Parade, April pre-1967. Pack leader Geoff Williamson, of the 23rd Croydon Scout Group, stands with his young companion in Katharine Street outside the Town Hall on the Park Lane side where the Mayor would be standing to take the salute. The scout marks the point in the march past where the 'eyes front' is signalled. Shorts were no longer worn as part of the uniform after 1967.

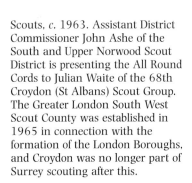

Scouts, c. 1963. Assistant District Commissioner John Ashe of the South and Upper Norwood Scout District is presenting the All Round Cords to Julian Waite of the 68th Croydon (St Albans) Scout Group. The Greater London South West Scout County was established in 1965 in connection with the formation of the London Boroughs, and Croydon was no longer part of Surrey scouting after this.

Swing boats at the Easter Fair at Coulsdon Common, April 1957. Coulsdon Common was acquired by the Corporation of London in 1883 and was described as 'having a most park-like appearance'. Over forty years later, in 1924 and 1926, Rydons Wood was added, and finally Merlewood. Two windmills were erected and demolished on the common, and farm animals once grazed the pasture. Sheep and cattle were reintroduced in 1990 to keep the scrub under control.

Sanger's Circus arrives for three weeks in Croydon, May 1930. This particular circus troupe had been coming to Croydon since around 1900. Local and national events like this were always very well attended by large crowds who would have watched the parade through the town before the circus reached its destination.

The Croydon Philharmonic Society Choir, conducted by Sir Edward Elgar, 1933. The choir has been in existence since 1914 and used to give concerts at the Civic Hall, North End, as well as at other locations. This three-concert event was one of the highlights in the choir's history. Sir Edward Elgar agreed to come and conduct a work of his own choice, *The Apostles*, and the choir performed with the London Symphony Orchestra. The soloists were Isobel Baillie, Astra Desmond, Eric Greene, Frank Phillips, Harold Williams and Arthur Cranmer. Two years later, in 1935, a four-day Elgar Festival was held to celebrate twenty years of the choir which is still active today.

CHAPTER SIXTEEN

SPECIAL OCCASIONS

The official opening of Coulsdon Boys' Club by HRH Prince Arthur of Connaught, seen here with Alderman Sir G. Broadbridge, 25 November 1935. The Boys' Club held their meetings where Coulsdon Youth and Social Centre is now, in Chipstead Valley Road. The hall is still used for meetings by young people's groups, including a Theatre Workshop and two Guide companies.

Lifeboat Day procession at the junction of Brigstock Road and London Road, July 1908. The two fund-raising processions (from the north and south of the borough) included mounted police, marching bands, various tableaux consisting of trailers pulled by horses, decorated cycles and handcarts and, of course, members of lifeboat crews. The afternoon was observed as a holiday in Croydon and schoolchildren were allowed to miss their lessons so they could join in the fun.

'Streets of Adventure' Carnival, Haling Park, August 1927. Len Wilkinson is seated wearing a sailor suit in the front row and his sister, Ivy, is behind him. The carnival was organised by the Croydon and District Traders' Association to raise money for Croydon General Hospital, and ran for many years before the outbreak of the Second World War. There was a street procession and decorated floats, fancy dress competitions, sports and even a baby show, all helping to make a memorable day out for around 20,000 Croydonians.

Queen Mary at Whitgift School, May 1938. Queen Mary presented new colours to the 4th Battalion, Queen's Royal Regiment. She was driven south through Norbury to the grounds of the school in Haling Park where she appeared 'a picture of regal beauty and dignity' according to a contemporary report in *The Croydon Times*.

Queen Elizabeth II visits Royal Russell School, March 1979. The Queen's visit (in a blizzard) marked the school's 125th anniversary. She made earlier visits in 1950, as Princess Elizabeth, to inaugurate work on new extensions, and in 1963 to inspect new buildings. The school was granted the prefix 'Royal' in 1953 to commemorate the school's centenary and the Queen's Coronation.

Diana, Princess of Wales' visit to Parchmore Methodist Church Youth and Community Centre, February 1983. Princess Diana asked to visit the Centre after hearing about an anti-boredom project for children held during the summer holidays. The Centre was established in 1968 to provide leisure opportunities for young people and has now become an important focus for community life in Thornton Heath. (*Reproduced by kind permission of the Croydon Advertiser Group.*)

A Coronation party in St Jude's Church hall, Thornton Heath, May 1937. The Coronation of King George VI, which had in fact been planned for his brother Edward VIII, was celebrated across the borough. Thousands of children were entertained at street parties, although heavy rain meant some of the celebrations had to be held indoors like this particular one.

A garden party given by Mr Thomas Hibbard Mason and his wife, Annie, Park Hill Rise, *c.* 1920. Mr Mason is seated in the centre of the front row with his dog. It would seem to be a rather more formal affair than most garden parties held nowadays! Mr Mason lived in East Croydon until 1937.

The London to Brighton Veteran Car Race, Russell Hill Road, Purley, November 1956. Crowds line the route as the cars pass by on their way to Brighton. Always a popular event, the Brighton Run, known initially as the Old Crocks Rally, has been in existence for over 100 years and often includes local entrants.

Woodcote Young Conservatives recruiting campaign, October 1958. Mrs F.N. Charlton is pictured 'launching' the campaign in Peaks Hill. The Woodcote group became Coulsdon Young Conservatives from 1968. There are no longer individual local Young Conservative Groups, they form part of the borough-wide organisation now.

A fancy dress parade in the grounds of Reedham School, c. 1920. This special event was organised by Purley Masonic Lodge, and local dignitaries dressed up to entertain the children. Reedham Orphanage took its name from the Revd Andrew Reed, who bought the site for an 'Asylum for Fatherless Children' to be built in 1853. Declining numbers of children in recent years, and the aging building, led to the decision to close the school where today there is a housing estate.

The Town Hall clocktower, illuminated for the Silver Jubilee of King George V and Queen Mary, May 1935. The programme of celebrations for the week included a civic banquet and ball, the presentation of mugs and beakers to schoolchildren, thanksgiving services, teas and entertainments for the elderly and a display of Jubilee Fireworks at Duppas Hill. A similar 'scheme of electrical illuminations' may have been used two years later for the Coronation of King George VI.

A street party celebrating the Silver Jubilee of Queen Elizabeth II, Wrights Road, South Norwood, June 1977. Street parties were held across the borough and everyone enjoyed the celebrations in spite of cool, wet weather. The residents of Wrights Road held their party the week prior to the Jubilee and were fortunate enough to enjoy sunshine. Carnivals were held, there were fancy dress parades and funfairs and people decorated their homes in honour of the occasion. (*Reproduced by kind permission of the Croydon Advertiser Group.*)

INDEX